D1757640

Worl

THE DROWNING OF THE SAINTS

THE DROWNING OF THE SAINTS

Paul Perry

salmonpoetry

First Published in 2003 by Salmon Publishing,
Cliffs of Moher, County Clare, Ireland
web: www.salmonpoetry.com
email: info@salmonpoetry.com

ISBN 1 903392 34 9

A CIP record for this title is available from the British Library.

Cover Artwork: *Tír na nÓg* by Eric Roux-Fontaine (mixed media and gold leaf
on paper). *Eric Roux-Fontaine is an international artist who lives between Ireland and
France. He is represented in Ireland by the Bridge Gallery in Dublin.*

Cover Design & Typesetting: Siobhán Hutson
Printed in Ireland by Colour Books

Salmon Publishing gratefully acknowledges the financial
assistance of The Arts Council/An Chomhairle Ealaoín

This book is for my family, and my friends

Acknowledgements

Acknowledgements are due to the editors of the following publications where these poems, or versions of them, first appeared:

Poetry Ireland Review, The Shop, Cyphers, Acorn, Three Candles Review, Poet Lore, Eire-Ireland, The Lightning Bell, The Hawaii Review, Callaloo, The Art Times, The Texas Review, The Dakota House, The West Wind Review, Poetry Midwest, The Drunken Boat, The Virtual Writer, TLS and *Scribner's The Best American Poetry 2000.*

Thanks to Allison Eir Jenks, Adam Zagejewski, Edward Hirsch, Mark Doty, Cynthia MacDonald, Fred D'Aguiar, C.D. Wright, Michael Harper, Joseph Lease, Christian Nagle, Daragh O'Toole, Aoife Ní Dhornáin, John Balaban, Fergus Kennedy and Mary Reynolds who provided invaluable insights and encouragement in the drafting of this book.

Thanks also to the Tyrone Guthrie Centre, at Annaghmakerrig and the Heinrich Böll House Committee for residencies where I worked on some of the poems.

Contents

Blessed is the fruit

Desolate apples, hold
tight in your bowl of water,
red, blushing, and blossoming light;

too big for the fruit bowl,
bitter pie stuff,
clean and eager

like some dowdy buoys
in a storm,
on say a Sunday,

and we wearing
our costumes,
not for mass,

but Halloween,
my brother remember is
something Frankensteinian

and I'm a ghost
dunking my head
into the cold

frivolous water
mouth open
like a dumb fish

in the depths –
childhood game;
apples, storm lights,

biblical beacons
of a lost faith,
first fruits, un–

forbidden, but lost
like round unanchored
islands where we

returned after walking
from house to house
and trundling to and from the bonfire

to where the bowl,
like two clasped
plastic pale green hands,

a memory turned over,
lay with its bitten and chewed,
that is the yellowing skin of apple flesh

swelling sadly into the soft
unforgiven pulp
of all consumed

and discarded
temptations, though this
was the first, the first I remember.

The morning after Halloween

"The English language belongs to us.
You are raking at dead fires..."
　　Seamus Heaney, "Station Island XII"

The morning after Halloween
the three boys returned
to where the fire had witched
in graceful, haunted movement
the night before.
A dolmen of fire.
Now they stood around the ring,
a dark patch of grizzled soil and ash,
stoking the last popping embers
to a shuffling flame.
From the window dreaming,
one of those boys is me:

we watch the rhythmic sway of the flame,
hypnotised.
The smoke rising black.
The spell peels, the wild
cracks and howls of the night before
smoulder with the dying flame
and the others go home to barmbrack
and a ten pence hidden in mashed potato.
If I could be that boy,
if that was me, I would stay
curious to witness
the ashen wood crumble
with the slightest hush of my breath.
Though I may have wanted to spark some flame
or found myself knee-dirty striking stone on stone,
I, too, left the fire and heard the wind

rise and saw the smoke
we had swallowed, like a voice
or the memory of a voice,
scatter and fade
over the desolate fields.

The Red Dogs of Wicklow

We walked the long road to Templeogue.
Trees lined the street,

their rheumatic joints aching dampness and cold.
We found the fox with its dank head

in a puddle, the dark rusty bristles of its fur
hardening into the wind like old nails.

I wanted to lift it over the wall
into a field where the grass and leaves

would discolour into its skin as it fell asleep
into the soil, remembering the red dogs of Wicklow

and their snow felt steps into the dark, outside our door.
But we were hesitant, unsure, afraid of disease

and cold with rain. Standing over the fox's body
with no benediction other than the thought

that things are passing from our lives. And so,
we walked on, with our own small hurts

to contend with, until we turned from Terenure
to Templeogue and by some magic I looked

behind to see the fox alive and skulking by a tree,
darting off, it seemed, in every direction possible.

Of the gas stove and the glimmerman

I'll have to ask some questions in the kitchen
of the picture hanging in the hall, of the thin pointing nose
and gentle eyes. I'll have to ask some questions

of the civil servant, of the stranger
with nine children. You must have left suddenly
without warning even to yourself.

You must have gotten up early for work
and forgotten stupidly to come home.
Silly man. Your presence is a gasp.

She, on the other hand, never forgets
a birthday. Christmas presents for everyone.
She tours her children's houses

like a ring leader or a small storm,
nodding her head and spreading gossip,
singing a song or two and dancing once in a while.

She's gas; her eyes hold the best
part of a century. She'll tell you about the Black 'n Tans,
Dev, the gas stove and the glimmerman.

She watches out for us all,
but as for you old man,
people don't talk about the dead.

You have long fingers,
did you play the piano?
The picture, of course, is in black and white

so that is how I imagine you
a character in a black and white movie,
dumb, except for your twirling umbrella,

and the words you might have uttered,
caught in her memory, escaping only occasionally
like the startled bass from a torn fishing net.

I'll have to invite a slip of the tongue,
a nostalgic wink, or a hushed splutter.
Rathfarnham has changed.

You must not have known Stillorgan, the 46A,
the bus she takes or the bombs that still
wake us, the debris of our independence.

Your presence is a gasp.
I ask Allison if I should even bother
scribbling these questions.

'Write about the silence,' she says.
Old man,
you must not have known

she would have taken care of you,
or that when her mother died
my parents were away,

that she walked to our house
to take care of us, her grandchildren,
until my parents returned

and said to them simply and sternly,
'We buried my mother today.'
I think about my parents fighting

about which of their parents
was more patriotic,
the guns under the shopping trolley.

I think of the car crash
when my mother lost a child
and the galaxy of questions we live under,

the sheds with private conversations,
and I think of you, looking at her
ironing your daughter's skirts

and their long hair too
before they ran out the door
to school and her, again, pressing a wet cloth down

onto the hot stove and steam rising,
in black and white, whenever she heard the step
of the glimmerman come softly.

Rhapsody with owl

the owl calls out like a gaping heart
and I am running plotting a getaway
through the wicklow fields
the building sites and lost wandering horses

maybe we knew they'd find us or maybe I did
or maybe my brother thought something different
maybe he really did think he'd get away
plotter and schemer that he was

with a black plastic bag
stuffed with jumpers and socks and jam sambos
my ankles were scabby and sore
from riding a new red bicycle I was sorry

to leave lying small and unconvinced
and shivering behind a bush
with no flames or sacrifice though the blackberries
were dripping with rain and that made them clean

and good to eat so that by the time
they found us our tongues were red like devils
my mother's car smelt of stale cigarette smoke
outside I smelt the freshly cut grass of summer

and heard the owl the dark glass sky
the fever the salt the thirst and colour
because the owl god of godless things
because the owl grass riddle glendalough

kilquade eight shadows from his mouth
because the owl feathered kafka glenmalure
airplanes and beetles candle flames
christ church no one is safe turned

around twice make any home your tree
any wind echo distance lack of water
or the sound thereof because the owl
black buddha of regret laughter in a well

small heart beat of forgiving wind thirst
salt the dark glass eye stars explode at your feet
the rain a dark web you are caught in
remember the sea is all around you

here is your past in a bowl take it
there is your future in the rain the sea
your face changed a thousand times into fire the soil
was red who are you petals of anger

in your palms lines paths I walked down
never turned left saw the rain and stars
death was on your lips on your tongue
in the air under rocks in the water

in your eyes on your lips again and when
you find yourself away gone into the new life
you did or did not imagine for yourself
how are you supposed to say that is who I am

that is where I am from when you've run away
into a world you do not even recognise
where dead dogs are thrown out with christmas trees
where the skies are orange and dusty wrecked

by thunder and tornadoes where the word home
makes you flinch and reminds you that all
runaways have the scar of failed attempts
like petty suicides on their lips

like a birthmark touched with a strange
curiosity where branches are swallowed
by the listening moon and flames are cupped
in hands here you spent yourself like a fever

to the house you once knew empty
derelict a body without belief where the walls
exhaled your name while you are perched
hunched wild-eyed before some small feast

of addiction like an angry owl pledging
your faith to the body body of the listening
moon still the two of us are running away
on a green cliff top in november

watching the waves wrinkle like birthmarks
in the night time rain through the muck
filled puddles with words skimming the water
of what we try to say like stones flung out

over the sea's expanse running
to the stray headlights of a mooring boat
down the driveway through the gate
into the laneway and the star-filled night.

The improbable flowers of Vizcaya

Outside, the fountains swallow the sun.
Again and again, I fall asleep
on Peacock Bridge
and dream of chasing kites

in my Italian childhood.
The living room replicates
a typical Renaissance room,
a high beamed ceiling,

a sixteenth century fireplace.
Plush coven.
Lumber room.
Loot.

The trees talk
in a prehistoric
gnarled and tangled
language. A two thousand

year old Roman tripod,
a fifteenth century Spanish
heraldic carpet.
Rococo ceilings

and two sixteenth century tapestries
depict the exploits of Hermes.
I want to sneak
into the butler's pantry.

No echo in my mouth.
Biscayne Bay, goodnight.
Beautiful Iseult, be with me
here, where the fishing boats

dawdle on the water
like small children
who should long have been asleep.
Here, we could walk

by the silk palm trees
with their gracious,
but improbable flowers.
You could say

you love me
and I would be Tristan
or whatever it is
you want me to be.

The Walk

after Chagall

I am a smear of lightning
over Barley harbour
briefly and writing to the sound
of rain is religion
my new blue singing religion
we took a walk
and grew too big for the town
we took a walk
over the hills the old fabric stitched hills
away from the town
out of the town the toy cornered town
it wasn't the wind
that took you into the sky
I held your hand
it wasn't the wind
I was happy or I was smiling
you flew like a kite
by my fingers and talked
about star apples
a fruit fallen from some far-off sky-past
a delicious edible pulpy mass
something to induce daytime visions

for days you wouldn't come down

On the avenue of the portal of angels

#4

there's been so little light today
for you, so little light
in one dream you were flying
a machine much like a house
in another a presence pressed down
onto the bed and leapt towards you
so you woke and spent the morning
thinking about conflicts which make
you who you are and time passing
once when you were on your way
to having your heart broken again
it's something you're trying to perfect
she said you've lost your calmness
and you could hear voices
from people and books
too much light can blind a person
the morning was like a flare
and now it has expired
all that is left is its hissing
after-birth and you are saying the words
there's been so little light today
I think of a poem like a beating heart
when your heart stopped
the lights went out

On the avenue of the portal of angels

#5

I didn't wake up
I was asleep all day
but still I arrived
a cloud with a treasure of rain
insisted

I saw the first snow drops of the year
in Forgney church
and promised to find some words
for the angel
who'd been following me

to feed the angel
I started with *snowdrop*
and suggested something from a life
I had led somewhere else
as a piece of parchment

onto which a phrase of gold chambered music
was inscribed
I became seasonal expectant
like one of those tiny pleasures
snowdrop

I know I need to contemplate
the vanishing moment
but this is not the time
when snow falls on snow
or one wave follows another

the angel's lips are drowsy
and I have promised
to feed it
with heavenbent dusks
and other pagan felicities

The Incredulity of St. Thomas

When he made love to a woman, the room is not important,
if there were a room, and the colour of her hair,
again unimportant, but red, that she was a stranger
may be of some consequence, in a town he had never
    before visited,

he looked into the woman's corn flower blue eyes, held her
firm beneath him and thought about the gravid night
when He appeared and bid him touch his wounds. He thought
about how his fingers had sought out the small cave

of flesh in the man's chest and how he had stumbled struck
with terror, how the calm sea of the soul was gone,
how waking dreams of snakes swallowing their own tails
followed him. What was wrong, she asked him.

He sat up, bemused, perhaps he looked out a window.
He might have seen an immensity of stars; he might
have sighed and thought how he could ask her whether
there were such things as forgiveness and redemption,

whether the night was but a veiled dream of desire,
whether his fingers had found anything other than longing.
He left the house, if it was a house, and the road was full
    of iridescent
dust, the heat made a tent of forgetting, the sun was falling

and he walked towards it, his mind opening like the unwalked
roads ahead of him. He did not ask himself whether the night
was the night or whether the woman standing in the doorway
was anything other than what it seemed, a twilight picture

with a moon hanging in the shape of a question mark,
but when after a time of walking he looked behind, he was not
surprised to find the town had already vanished, hidden behind
a cloud of dust or lost perhaps in the ravenous thicket of stars.

To Dexter Above

i.m. of Dexter Gordon

I picture you playing an old ballad
say *I guess I'll hang my tears out to dry*
in some god-awful after-life cellar
teaching the angels to swing, those patient
white winged students waiting for the shabby
saxophone to start its praying, chipped
and dented, bedraggled gold like the sun-
light hazy, weak and sweet on those early
mornings in Paris, restless, unsleeping,
lost wanderings with junk and alcohol
beating through your blood, your eyes dark marbles
of loving suspicion, a face of ash,
itinerant fingers of exile, wry
shadow, old one time actor you paced
your way on grooves and glissandos full of
sound and fury, full of love and loss and
made beautiful burnished labyrinths
of sound, your gray lips, which you once dreamt bled
like the reed and your mouth and your lips all
blood, viscous velvet pain, wordless phrases,
expelling all the wonderful regrets
of our lives and when you make the horn talk
up there in your new home, in our night sky
the stars appear like startled orphans still
celebrating the wedding of brass and
wood, the luscious reed, how many thousands
did you lick and split in the blue frenzy
of hopeless dream-catching, in a sorry
attempt to conjure twilight, your inspired
improvisations opened like a long
letter to the night asking it to take

you and though our ideas of heaven may
be far too simplistic, because to bar
the blues from paradise would be nothing
less than blasphemy, the tenor of your
voice, gravel and dark, would not complain,
but blow the blue note and *Go* like an ever
enduring soul bark into the eternal night.

The heretic that makes the fire

What if this broken pale alabaster
had once been flesh, had once
felt the warm night air, and what
if these cold pursed lips were about
to say something, say, release a kiss,
and what if this bodice of cracked
stone were some kind of saint,
or like Hermione was about to speak,
what would it say, and what
you want to know, what kind
of person could have chiselled
such longing in stone, a longing
for god perhaps, or love,
though with the absence of two
clasped hands you wonder could
this hapless nomad of masonry
still believe in sin, for it is not
marble, nor gilded, but maybe it,
I mean you, can help, maybe if I
stay by your side and pray to you
before the sea takes you back,
maybe then I can be forgiven,
the way an unconvincing memory
is remembered, as if some parts
of us belonged to someone else,
forgiven for my own private
failures, not that I want to be
dipped in the River Lethe, but
what if this small feast of stone
could resuscitate itself and this is
the trick of the imagination,
albeit with a fever, and say to me
forgiven, but you won't, will

you, you will look dumbly at me,
you will say change your life,
you will leave me to wonder
if only time could slow down
and did not race away from us
and leave us confused at the day's
forays, leave us like sleepwalkers,
as I am now before you, kindling
your image like a heretic that makes the fire
and muses what wasteful war
brought you or were you thrown
from the armada by a mariner
priest, what ship went to ground
that you are washed up like this,
wet sand dousing your leg,
did you despair with the body,
are your lips chipped because
language could not articulate
your desire to be something
more, more permanent than
wasting flesh and what if you
are a sign, but that is what you are, isn't it?

The Straw Mannequin

after Goya's painting of the same name

they think it funny
what they're doing to me
they laugh
they think it hilarious
hysterical creatures
my four sisters
my four wives
four women
I don't know
strangers they are
sirens if you like
how they found me
I don't know
look at them
made up like
a troop of tarts
dolls and as for what
they've done to me
tied me to a post
in McFadden's field
and filled my shirt
and pants with straw
took me home
after four days
without sleep
and painted me up
like a clown
I was weak
hallucinating
they took the sheet
off my bed

and carried my
weightless body
to the field
where they're throwing
me now up and
down like a
toy a plaything
a pet my neck
is limp out of joint
like a puppet's
my limbs jangling
like a set of soundless
keys my cheeks
are rouged and the sky
closes in and falls
away closes in
and falls away
I am weightless
and they laugh
and their laughter
arrests all other
sounds it fills
my head so I
can think of
nothing
of where I'd been
or who I was before
this charade began
or why I deserve
their derisive
hilarity
their shrill chortles
the four women's
strong as ox

flinging me
towards that lucent
crack in the sky
if only I could
make it to be
away from
their laughter
which fills my head
and the sky
and takes the voice
from every
wingéd thing

Tonight, the sea

'No blame can be attached with certainty to the native Irish who
undoubtedly witnessed the wrecks, the captures and the hangings,
except perhaps to point out that no attempt was made to aid the
Spaniards of whom not one survived.'
Niall Fallon, from *The Armada in Ireland.*

Tonight, the sea calls out
to all souls shipwrecked or not.
Tonight, the sea wends its way into your thoughts,
its dark green skin beckoning to embrace you
over distances of geography and time
urging you to imagine an armada of drowned sailors
to witness a barrage of ghosts
smouldering upward into the bruised halo of the moon.
Tonight, the sea calls out
and you are here circling Cnoc na Crocaire,
poor witness watching
the shadows ride the dark tracks of night
and the rain shoot down
into a scaffold of grief,
listening to the lament of the waves
working the past into a frenzy of surf,
envisioning the fear the mariners felt.
But really, what can you do? Stand,
shiver on the shore and ruminate?
Is there anything to salvage from this sea?
This is all a gesture of longing.
Imagine the fear they felt, Spanish and Irish alike.
Do what the sea tells you to do,
take the words like loot
and write of a carved cabin door
from the Santa Maria de la Rosa
which became a carved cabin door in O'Connor's farm
or an oak table with a mahogany top

from the San Juan Bautista which became an oak table
with a mahogany top in Dromoland Castle.
Write about small bounties of loss,
how saints and sinners went down
with the elemental pull of calamity.
Witness the sea and watch
as it lowers the sky, pulls down the clouds
and makes a symphony of cliff and stone
with its briny absolutions, its declarative waves,
its voices and chants, its swallowed anchors
and quilted face of nets and pots and sinking stars.
Be here tonight, and listen as the sea calls out
to all souls shipwrecked or not,
stand accounted for, and watch
while to the sea's aid like a thousand
wrecked dawns a storm hurries.

Ode to a Banjo

You need to wait for the silence
the silence snow commands.

You need to find yourself
obsessed and not with a woman.

I'm thinking of a soldier
from the Irish Brigade,

deserter, court-martialed,
listening on his last night

to a banjo with its bones
made of ghosts, poker faced,

goat-hide, wound, spell,
magic word, stamping

the gravely ground down,
a twisted ankle, from Donegal

to Down South.
There's something of the river

in the quiver of the strings,
cold on the feet as you step

in, and it's dusk or dawn
and the banjo with a moon for a head

is fading in the far off sky
where you are running,

your scent dispersing among the trees,
your childhood rising like smoke.

Far off you can hear it,
digging the soil, somewhere

in the forest, tempting
the scaffold with a body,

the snow's silence corrupted.
And the man who plays

the sodden tune, no one
calls him by his name.

In the Country Where It Is Always Winter

After Pieter Breughel's *Hunters in the Snow*

I am tired of romping in this cold beauty
in a land without memory where the wind and the snow ...
I am tired of the voluptuousness of winter.
This town is unfamiliar, not even as close as a cousin.

The sky is a dishevelled grey. The same pale colour
as my brothers' eyes. What they are thinking? I don't know.
We have longed since ceased to communicate.
What use? It does not stop our wanderings.

It does not help us to escape this country.
The country where it is always winter.
That these dogs are starving like the ragged souls of this town
does not surprise me. Did I say brothers?

At one time they were strangers, but when
that was I can't say. And the dogs too, vagabonds,
strangers themselves, immune to disease.
They follow us as if we had anything for them.

You'd think they would run to the fire, but
warmth of that kind is an illusion. What kind
of purgatory is it when the town's people skate on
ice? A town called temptation? If only we could stay here.

If only there were some kind of salvation in the snow.
The sound of the fire, dumb like the dreamless nights of sleep.
The children's voices I can hear, echoes in a well.
As for the swallows their immaculate twisting rends nothing.

And the dogs, the dogs, no whimpering for these mutts.
Just a slow sifting of the white ground.
Their anxious feet make the snow a poor betrayer
to the silence, a silence that rises like the dank

smell of smoke. A silence I have become used to.
Hoary and full of echoes. I want to say I left a loved one behind,
but I can't. Maybe I did, but I don't know now.
It's been so long. I imagine what she would have looked like.

But that again is another impossible task.
I can't get beyond the hands. A chilly alabaster, slender.
One last look onto the ice then.
Ice so hard I can almost dream of another life beyond its surface.

It carries our stern reflections as we descend.
Look, the trees stand with a wracked and solitary anguish.
They are like brittle black skeletons in the on-coming twilight.
And like windmills the children wave their innocent arms.

Letters to a Stranger

Dropped like stones
into a well
without water. A diary
of sorts, lost and unread.
Words which tell
little, remaining unopened.
Like a voice and its dark,
a buried mirror,
an echo in a scrap metal well.
Like a tentative knock
on the door of the spirit.
Dear you,
I have written these letters
without a reply
to a house where a few
trees have reached over. Here,
they have ached in slow deliberation,
urging,
desperately trying to convene
some kind of communication.
If anything only to suggest,
with their slow sound,
do not return. In the hallway
of the house, the letters still lie,
each signature a careful wound.

The Seducer's Diary

for Harry Clifton

As you were going backwards
Through the Brenner, I was coming out
The other side ... dawn, a field
Scarpered in mist. Copenhagen.
A train tumbling through the landscape of desire.

A man from Senegal mumbled
The Koran, as if to say the spirit
Wants to reproduce itself, to pro-create.
Yes, he should have married Regine.
Socrates had his shrew, Xanthippe.

I, too, was unprepared for the perpetual
Daylight of desire. The sardonic smile
Falls from his lips like a man jumping
From a cliff as the steps crumble behind him.
He does not shake his head, but holds it

In his hands. Regine for him was Schlegel.
'Will you never marry me?' Poor Regine.
The pseudonym will not save him,
Even if the diary helped him escape.
Think of lightning from a hill

In Budapest, if you like, where the ghost
Of Sandor might have walked. Wine
Cannot save you or churches or spires.
But, Harry, I do not think he walked away
From the flesh as easily as you imagine.

What nymphets, what spiritual flesh
Tempted him to teach her the erotic?
We cannot know. One prostitute was all
He had. His soul, a lantern wavering
In the darkness. His dilemma is ours.

The wanting spirit. Imagine he had
Taken a train to the body. Think
Of the lightning in his chest and the surprise
When he found himself stepping off
The train into another city, another life.

Conjugation of a Mirror

While you are walking through Chicago
saying good-bye to an old lover
I am indoors tracing a small chain
of indefatigable ants on my arm.

I stand in the porch
and watch the rain tumble down
from the cupped leaves of palm trees outside.

Scraps of paper are washed away.
I can see you tripping along your favourite streets,
wondering what will happen to us in the future.

Early morning light startles my eyes.
A glass of water, and the quiet
arrival of a day without you.
I begin to notice the slowness in things.
The trees own time in the wind,
voices washing in and out of each other.

There's not enough space on my desk
for what I am trying to do.

The day remains dumb.

Night scratches at the doors and panelling.
Another downpour.

I throw more poems out everyday, and bread

for the birds. Nothing much happens
this time of night.
A siren, and next door's singing.

Yes, I have been reading, and music too.
Upstairs the businessman comes home drunk again.

I imagine you there, sitting in some jazz club,
replaying old grooves, swing lover,
bashing out more poems everyday,
changing your clothes compulsively.

While I am here, my wings full of water,
asking the same questions about swans,
and lights and dark roads, dreams
scampering down alleyways.

You'll come back with tangled birds in your hair,
dirty fingered rosaries,
with spilt drinks, and unlit candles.

I'll be here with forgetting's dull lamp in the corner,
trying to pierce autumn's red alphabet
with my own tangled dreams,

rusted a little by Wednesday's rain.

from the valley of dry bones

Berlin to Dublin, 1945

—sotto voce—

1.

A plush girandole spluttered above the rooftops. *Pray. Dream.*
Boots nuzzled the loose scree. *Dream again.* Luck. A lantern
swung anxiously. *On the ferry. You told me. To pray.* Where my
bones mumbled. *Dream. You are lucky.* About the winter.
Thank you. A dwarf poured his lament into the wind. *One of
the few. To be allowed.* While in the street a woman's eyes said:
Why. Thank you. I am going to open your graves and let you live.

2.

And the discarded wings of angels.

Tell me: there is nothing you need to know.
There is nothing you need to know.

A boat without oars jostles on the water.

Every time I want to tell you something,
what happened on my way here,
you say: take this like a bribe. Rain fell like fire burning.

Burns slow like green wood. A funeral. In a harbour.
Where swans.
Or like a glance at a clock that does not tell the time.
Like green wood burning.
Slowly. Never actually arriving. Like swans.
In a harbour. A funeral.

The words found like a horseshoe fallen
from the hoof of an old knackered horse.

Tell me: there is nothing you need to know.
There is nothing.

I have owed you this feeling since ... March.

This digging a hole. A small forgiving.

The words, a horseshoe hanging above the lintel.

There were nights when none of us spoke.
The speaking was all around us.

A tree. Money. The gutted night. A boat without oars.
Fingers crawling
across the country of the face. Fruit to catch.

Take this like a bribe. Rain fell like fire burning.
And angel figures. In a harbour.
Lanterns. Boots. A horseshoe. Like green wood.
Or a girandole.
Swans.

Your eyes so full of winter.

3.

your dizzy refuge   a memory   remade in rain
like the wind through the teeth of a swinging gate   a river
in the rain swathed   in rumour   in unanchored light
a river   or crabs   crawling from their harbour walls
a city   in mirrors   the echo of people talking   boots
a river through glass   in a mirror   in a river   in a well
a frog   a dead blue tit   like wind   or crabs in a harbour
people   remade   in rain   echo   the stars
you wore   like rusted anchors   into the sea

the marks on the body

a pale march sun
rises on my arm

birthed by your lips
your teeth

the marks on my body
scratchings and bruisings

a menagerie of faded yellows
a recipe of purpling blues

and truculent black
from your lips

healing slowly
from your hands

blossoming on my neck
blooming impermanent

tattoos of your desire
different to the three

you wear flourishing
and flowering on

my shoulder blades gifts
unlike the ones you received

as a woman with child
by a boy who called you his own

I scour your body
with my mouth I cover

every scar and wound
healed or hidden

I take away
the pain as best I can

Looking for beauty in a crab pool

shiver   water

skin of another

you have
so much to tell me

I know
I know
so much to tell me

shiver water

one crab
eating   another

River of Light

red, green and yellow neon
blur the highway
into a river of light

the intersection appears
like a mirage
smoke wafting from the policemen's flares

call them mourning candles
three a.m.
surrounding the scene

the intersection
like a small island of sorrow
the car should not

be cut in half
so easily, so simply
but it is, there

we watch, dumb spectators,
held back
by yellow tape

as the police measure
confer and agree
the yellow plastic

covering the unnamed dead
flaps in the wind
like an ignominious flag

a warning, a reminder
flapping absurdly in rhythm
with the smashed blinker

of the halved car,
again yellow
until the ambulance appears

and departs, easily, simply
the shattered glass swept away
the car removed

the tape taken
so that everything
looks as it did

an hour before
when we passed
on the other side

an unending kaleidoscope
a blurring, ever-moving
river of light

fill the room with lilies

there's not enough time
in your dreams I know

relax for god's sake take it easy
there's time enough to taste

to breathe slower and look back
you hurry through your life

that's why it goes so fast
wait wait think of the jar you wrapped

your tiny fingers around as a child
and the garden you stumbled through

and the fireflies that danced in the jar
think about when you set the jar down

think about long walks without thought
put whatever it is aside

the stars tremble
tell them to stop and forget for a minute

that your mother never held you
when she should have

think of the rain
in the afternoon in Miami

its warm subsiding
its calm after-breath

like Sunday afternoons
and our love-making

ignore the car alarms
the crying child's not yours

brush your hair if you need to
tell me to do it but quietly

what it is the night wants from you
forget forget too the malls highways

turnpike bills and car crashes
close your eyes to the palm trees the storms

and neon gods inhale slowly
our precious life and if for some reason

the night decides to keep me
and I have not touched your face

or brushed against your lips
on that particular day forgive me

forgive me and fill the room with lilies
scatter our words through the air

and remember the basement in Chicago
how I held you in our poverty

and if there is a time when you run to me
with a new poem and forget that I am not there

do not fret you know what I would have said
think of the day when we circled the lakes at Como

how you hung on tight
on the back of that old motorbike

how we made it back to the pension
before the sky opened and the storms

you adore came think of us love
in some kind of final embrace

on the balcony watching the world
crumble and fall before us

Sundays

First, you had to wear your Sunday best,
say a stiff navy blue shirt, ironed trousers,
slacks your father called them. Your shoes
you had to polish. You and your brother

bent over in the kitchenette, your mother
said *utility* room, rubbing the old yellow rag
over the football worn leather,
the laces you tried not to pull too tight

made brittle by winter's shrug. Next you would have
to find your father's keys, lost, misplaced,
hidden. A frantic escapade under cushions
and clocks where you stood about looking

in places twice, thinking already about the end
of mass, hoping he wouldn't catch you idling
and when the keys, sacrosanct themselves, were found
and you didn't have to help pour a kettle of steaming

water onto the frost inscribed windscreen of the car
you crowded into the back seat where the ascetic sting
of his after-shave waited with the thin lips
of his impatience. Your mother was giving it, mass,

a miss this week. Later, when you became an altar
boy, you were seduced by the language of faith:
the *sacristy*, a mysterious and alluring word you
relished like *tabernacle* or *liturgy*, cold on the tongue

like iron. *Chalice* had the reassuring inflection
of an austere dawn and all the authority and apparent
order that incited reverence like the chilling command
of a parent, as if the words were a punishment you

were thankful for. Men shuffled from foot to
foot at the back of the church like cattle
trying to shake the musty dank of their breed,
restless for the other public house to open.

The wind hustled its way
through the doors upsetting the tranquillity
of the candle flames where old women knelt.
You shuffled your way into the heavy oak pews

and sat and stood according to the priest's directions,
all the time looking at the girl in the seat in front of you,
her bare supple neck revealed as something
blessed and while St. Paul wrote to the Corinthians

you thought about devouring the flesh before you.
And then there hung poor Jesus on the cross alone.
When it came time to take communion
you mulled over whether to take it in your hand

or directly into the mouth and once you overcame
that one quandary you worried over how not to sink
your teeth into the body of Christ, something your brother
told you would send you straight to you know where.

It felt strange to have swallowed his body,
to have consumed the son of god,
to implicate yourself in something
which sounded like a crime, *transubstantiation.*

Outside the church after mass
your father gave you money, a pile of dirty coins,
to buy the newspapers and you waded home,
the headlines smearing your fingers with ink

and after dinner, maybe your grandparents were along,
before your father settled into his arm-chair,
you wondered briefly
what it was he might have prayed for,

whether he thought about Jesus alone on the cross,
whether he too was afraid of the dark
when the heavy oak doors of the church closed
and the candles, with a quiet gasp, were quenched.

Apologia

I wake to the sound of sirens
and stillness across the street
fire engines tumble away
to the fires of my imagining

if you look out the window
our neighbour Desiree
a name I've heard called out into the cold night
is being taken away

the first day we met her
her teeth sticking to each other
she told us we lived in the Galleria-ghetto
the poor among the rich

the previous tenant had been shot
dead in our front yard
nothing newsworthy not these days
I took the fridge she said without apology

but where will you go Desiree
now that you have no home
and where will red dog live
the birds argue about other matters

they turn the trees' leaves to a jubilee
and look the yellow lilacs are out of control
the pond I tried to dig in the back
a grave you called it is filled with water

the summer is on its way
you can smell it
welling up in the tough grass
another year tunnels its way to star-filled July

one of the cats you suspect is pregnant
frogs quake in road-side puddles
hundreds of them what am I to pray to
now that god has left me

the bar at the end of the street is sleeping
its neon in the morning looks dazed
I stop praying and start writing poems
apologias for not having lived a better life

notes to make me calm take stock
make lists and listen
closely to the interval between alarm bells
words to help me think about the car that passed

our house late last night and the shot
that was fired words to make me wonder
about that flare that golden hand
in the night and what it was reaching for

Seven Days in Chicago

Day 1.

On the first day
you said let there be pain
and there was

I've been whispering
the ghost of fires

drowning wake up
or let me into your dreaming
here my admission ticket

four charred fingers anything
burnt or broken a blue flame

how can I stop you from turning

I begin to burn

I'm not myself
I'm no one

I have to tell myself to stop wanting

the sky
to fall into your shoes

in the morning the wind
wants you

if it wasn't for people turning to stone

if it wasn't for dark bodies
or dilapidated hearts

Day 2.

I want to know
what the water is saying

retreating

I am jealous of you and the night
you're closer

the moon's in on it too

the trapdoor moon
you keep pushing me through

you cling to stolid Floridian palms

blindfold me

I've given you more than words

you want all the pain to be yours
but childishly I bruise
like the clouds at dusk

teach me how to love you
tell me how

you like to play Ophelia

I'm neither here nor there

busy with grief
like spiders in a pot

a wasp's nest

Day 3.

I wait for any sign

the babbling voice not mine
the words not mine

talk to the night
persuade it to be something else

someone else

two green bananas
from the small tree
outside the house

I'm so hurt
I can't talk

did I learn this from you

the violence inside us

I sit under the sausage tree
waiting for the saxophones

to start their praying

you are there
slow eyed talker

two names pen-knifed
into that stodgy old oak

your face in the bronze water
my fingers paralysed
inchoate

a mess of light
this our blunt effort at love

Day 4.

pale morning smells
honeysuckle eucalyptus

children in a playground
running like crazed ants

your dizzy life
making me sea-sick

goodmorning
to your soft pale skin
goodmorning

above your birthmark
your knee is bruised and swollen

I grow into the swelling
my fingers and my eyes

to be waking with you
the faint memory of you

I reach out of sleep
to be waking with you

from one dream into another
like opening a door

to the same room always
waking with you

the faint memory of you

Day 5.

let me guide you
come with you
now that I have no home

you come to bed
your clothes
lie
on the ground
without your body
where you left them

if you listen
to what we were dreaming
I am ready to rest

anywhere

red lake wind burning
coconut dragonfly
dancing over tadpoles
the shadow of a lizard
on scrap-metal

or the bells in Gründelwald

how can I hold you
with all your hurt
the desolate shaking

keeping us awake

I would have preferred a simple life
a life with simple things

Day 6.

I am aching in your muscles
in the murmur of your body

if you find my soul
in the lost and found

taste it
slowly

the healing

that's what it said the insouciant wind

perhaps it was Tír na nÓg
this recurring dream
when Oisín fell from his horse

I think of Inis Mór
repeating to myself
that I wanted this silence
to empty the head

if it had not been for the week

or the blue songs
we could have been anywhere

but we were neither here nor there
we were busy with grief

like spiders in a pot

Day 7.

There was no seventh day.

Paris

homage to Celan

Make me bitter.
Count me among the almonds.
Drink
From my mouth.

Count me among the almonds.
The night is the night.
From my mouth
You almost would have lived.

The night is the night.
In the swell of wandering words.
You almost would have lived.
Without words too.

In the swell of wandering words.
You fill the urns and feed your heart.
Without words too.
Twelvemouthed.

And I lie with you, you in the refuse.
Get drunk and name yourself Paris.
Twelvemouthed.
As if we could be we without us.

Count me among the almonds.
Make me bitter.
You almost would have lived.
Make me bitter.

Oisín

a nightmare I drowned
a beehive was I in Spain
mills and oranges
an afterlife

I started to swallow
bones blind men
surrounded me
I was a boy with different coloured eyes

from somewhere originally
there were no faces
but numbers and months
a perpetual november of the soul

and here are your pockets
cul de sacs with stones
and old lovers so this is hell
a funeral again and again

the priest is turning the corner
turning the corner
dropping the chalice
they never played

the music you asked for
Liszt Hosanna
what's her name
men know about the soil

enough to fill their mouths with it
the country the city then hell
I never used to believe
my voice

was an echo in a well
never leaving my chest
I'm supposed to push
through this door

push through
I'm as afraid as when I was alive
I take a deep breath
I push through the door

I hear the bucket fall into the well

The Ring

We bought it in a pawn store
on Westheimer. We were already
married a year. You wanted
to wear it right away and not
wait on the charade I had planned.
You were right.
I wondered sometimes
whose ring it was before
it became ours, or yours,
how had it found its way
into the pawn store,
a small diamond,
among all the televisions,
video recorders, camcorders,
cameras, knives, jewellery,
pornography and guns.
Later, when it had all gone wrong,
when we had gone wrong,
when you had turned up without
the ring to take the furniture
that was yours, it was all yours,
I noticed the absence,
but said nothing. That night
I found the receipt
by the bedside table, no
note, just the ring's receipt
and I thought about it,
the ring, returned to where
it waited, to where it belonged.

Slowly Home

take the third train east
use no whips or spurs
but a gentle whisper
to encourage the driver

say good-bye to all you've known
but slowly, you have time
don't talk to your taxi
or pretend to be someone else

if the old guy takes you
on a detour, say nothing
smile politely, if you should
arrive in a strange land

where people no longer talk the tongue
you once knew, simply nod
and thank your fare
do not ask for directions

the stars obviously are not themselves
the headlines you suspect are a decoy
people leer at you conspiratorially
if you walk the streets

and you do not recognise them
no matter, if you happen
to stumble into a back-garden
weakly resembling a photograph

you once carried in your wallet
welcome the place with open arms
and the family that come now to greet you
take them, too, as your own

Leap Year Lake

at the asylum seekers support group meeting
where after three weeks the caring committee members
have still not come up with a name
for the party and have wrankled over the words
for its mission with painstaking deliberation

I think of it, leap year lake,
the joy in just saying it, the lake
we passed on our way to Moydow,
after an afternoon of poetry in Virginia,
a palm of water which was not there,
hidden like an innuendo, or an unspoken
thought, curled up into some arid underground fist,

assumed though that it would arrive,
like a rumour
or a slur, the kind you hear on Dublin street
about our guests, who are bored and crammed
and live under direct provision
which itself sounds like a sentence
to serve under

we are careful about what we say
in the constitution to the unnamed support
group for those who have arrived from other places
and may have names we can't pronounce and faces
we have not yet recognised

it's there as the politics and rhetoric
makes me dizzy an image of the lake arriving
like a black bead in a rosary of reds or blues
and the water, its water, the lake's,
leap year lake's water

is like a dark spell the sky has cast,
its own secret reflection,
a beautiful disappearance elected to arise
once every four years, but by whom,
or by what, a common syntax or better yet
a language perhaps
which suggests sustenance, breath, life, our wish
to return always to where we started from,
to be present always, even when we are not
or cannot be

with the rain, which has created a season of itself
and which punctuates the lake's return
leap year lake
go on imagine you are there
by its banks now
pushing your memories out
like a boat
not with a name, an agenda,
but with an exhalation and a mysterious plangent
grammar, nominated, seconded, at once unanimous.

The bats at Annaghmakerrig

We had our backs
against the wall
and watched like sins
thrown to a storm
the bats whirring
and spinning the hours
before dawn
into a tale we took
hold of and up and down
close to the face, a
breath, dizzying the dark
like leather winged devils
postponing the morning,
blind adepts of the night
death has sent out
like inky toys to be
worshipped by our
sleepless eyes until
their winding slowed
and they retreated
leaving the two of us
by the wall closing
our eyes to the light,
our ears to their sound,
heartbeat to nothing.

A cemetery outside Chetumal

the sun calls shadows
into dull salmon coloured walls
telegraph poles topple the sky

the longer the dead have been here
the faster you need to walk
Chac's face burns

through the battered sanguine gate
dusty angels laugh
our footprints away

echoes of themselves
hyacinth blue tombs
bloom in clay

words catch
in your throat
we're incidental and I know

what you're going to say:
save yourself
the sky storms, a red totem

admit it we're lost
and in more ways than one
walking up and down

like dumb clowns
scared out of our wits
for a rainstorm

while in the hills
there are more deaths
than you claim your bones have borne

Ferry from Gotland

the crows are at my head again
a murder of them
wet and scrawny
milk and water
and dreams of gunpowder
flitting away another future

they haunt me
the ghost ships

a dream again
my life is made up of night time visions
a pier,
horses, flesh and blood and metal
carousing us into the water
and then onto an island
transformed

the footsteps, their echoes
are ours, again

night falls like the rain
again and again

darkening the way between our hearts

I thought my dreams would change

waves made of voices

too quickly the moment is gone

strange to see the medieval
revellers, teenagers in costume,
reliving something from so long ago –
their imitations are not even echoes

history is a party
invitation only

sounds to me like god-land
heaven's alibi

Maria, Maria

if you see a light in the distance
let it be me
coming towards you
a beacon
bringing you home

The Gate to Mulcahy's Farm

The gate to Mulcahy's farm is crooked,
sinking into infirm soil like a ship
from the Spanish Armada if you like,
forged and felled in some dark cave

to find itself jaded with flaking eroded gilt
leaving the striations prison-like,
shaded a coppery green. A gate without
a handle and unlike all others in any

neighbouring field without the dull sanguine
frame that swings to and fro like a hinge,
or a door itself to some other world.
No, this is no ordinary gate and there is

something majestic in its stolid refusal
to swing, something absurd even.
Perhaps this is another version of heaven,
imagine the bedroom it might once have graced,

this brass headboard, this discarded,
transported remnant of love's playground,
and look, two golden and intact globes
rest on either end, both transcendental transmitters,

receivers maybe of rough magic,
piebald love, communicating not sleep,
sleep no more, but wake, wake here
to the earth and imagine if you want

the journey of such an armature
of fecund passion, what hands gripped
these bars, what prayers were murmured
through the grate of this ribald cagery?

Imagine too the man who must have
hurled and pitched and stabbed
this frame into the ground, in a dark rain of course
after his wife had died, her passing to us unknown

though you know this
that there must have been some act
of violence within this frame-work,
some awful, regrettable pattern caught

in the form of what? Wind rushing through a brass
headboard, an exclamation point to the querulous
division of fields, could we be talking border-country,
and the broken, airy, moss-eaten stone walls.

Think about when the farmer died and the farm
was sold, think about what happened, the field, empty
of its cows, still with its stones and grey soil,
maybe this is Monaghan,

maybe some day it, the brass headboard
you are looking at now, will be sold
to an antiquarian in a Dublin shop,
brought there on a traveller's horse and cart,

not smelted down or disassembled, but sold
to a store where some lady with a wallet
will buy the thing, the elegant shabbery before you
that is the gate to Mulcahy's farm. As for the bed

itself, we can speculate, let it have sunken
into the earth, or better still let the earth be the bed,
the cot, mattress and berth to this sinking headboard,
this beautiful incongruous reliquary of misplaced passion.

After the Cabaret

After Emmy Hennings

Early morning I head for home.
The clocks strike five, it'll soon be bright.
Though the light in the hotel still burns,
The cabaret is finally over.
In a corner children cower,
The farmers are already on their way to the market.
People go to church, quiet and old.
From towers the bells ring out earnestly,
And a prostitute with wild hair
Still wanders around, cold and without sleep.

Love me of all my sins clean.

You see, many's the night I've kept my vigil.